Creating a Successful Change Plan for Projects and Organisational Transformation

Step-by-Step Instructions, Tools and Templates

Ira Bayborodina

Table of Contents

Introduction

Hello, my name is Ira Bayborodina, and I'm excited to share my journey and expertise with you in this book on change management. With extensive experience in project and program management in New Zealand, I ventured into the realm of change management a few years ago. However, I quickly realised that finding a comprehensive and user-friendly guide to change management activities was a challenge.

Undeterred, I embarked on a journey of research, learning and experimentation. Through extensive research and hands-on experience, I developed my tools, methodologies and step-by-step processes for navigating change effectively. The result is a collection of practical insights and strategies that I've gathered and refined over the years.

In this book, I aim to fill the gap I encountered by providing a clear and comprehensive guide to change management activities. My goal is to offer a resource that is not only easy to follow but also rich in theoretical and practical wisdom and actionable steps. By sharing my tools and methodologies, I hope to empower others in their change management endeavours and enable them to succeed in their projects and organisational transformations.

I believe that effective change management is essential for driving meaningful and sustainable change in any organisation. By equipping professionals with the knowledge and tools needed to navigate change confidently, I hope to make a positive impact on individuals and organisations alike.

Thank you for joining me as we embark on this change management journey, and I hope you find the book valuable and inspiring.

Creating a Successful Change Plan: Step-by-Step Instructions, Tools and Templates

When embarking on a change plan for your project, you need to consider a set of key steps and principles. This guide is designed to walk you through the essential steps and tools necessary for effective change implementation. Whether you choose to utilise all available tools or only a select few depends on the complexity of your project. Given the unique nature of each project, organisation and level of change involved, it's important to customise your approach accordingly to ensure optimal results.

Navigate the Steps Described in This Guide

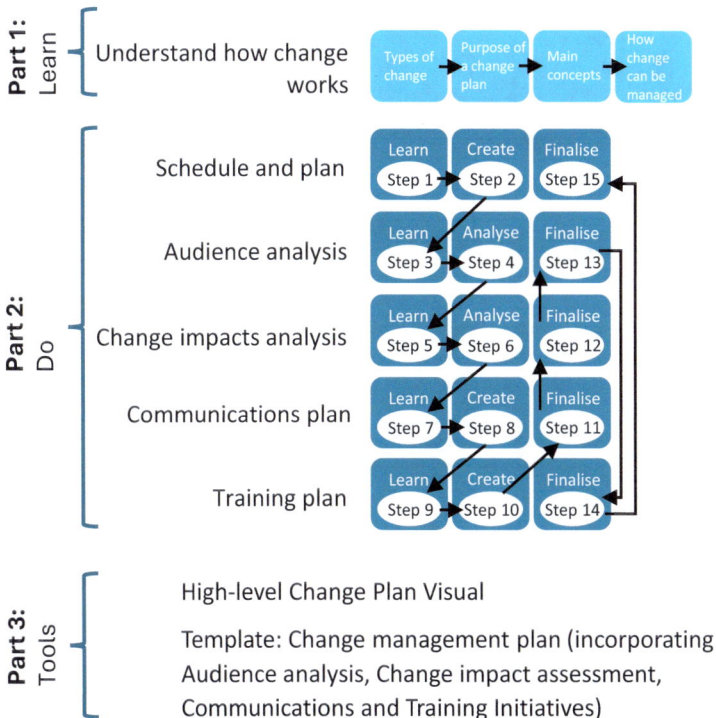

Part 1: Learn

Understand how change works

| Types of change | Purpose of a change plan | Main concepts | How change can be managed |

Part 2: Do

Schedule and plan

| Learn Step 1 | Create Step 2 | Finalise Step 15 |

Audience analysis

| Learn Step 3 | Analyse Step 4 | Finalise Step 13 |

Change impacts analysis

| Learn Step 5 | Analyse Step 6 | Finalise Step 12 |

Communications plan

| Learn Step 7 | Create Step 8 | Finalise Step 11 |

Training plan

| Learn Step 9 | Create Step 10 | Finalise Step 14 |

Part 3: Tools

High-level Change Plan Visual

Template: Change management plan (incorporating Audience analysis, Change impact assessment, Communications and Training Initiatives)

Types of change	Purpose of a change plan	Main concepts	How change can be manage

Learn:

Understanding Types of Project and Organisational Change

Learn: Understanding Types of Project and Organisational Change

Organisations may undergo various kinds of change, each with its characteristics and implications. Below, you will find the common types of change occurring within organisations or projects:

Strategic change: Strategic change involves significant shifts in an organisation's mission, vision, goals or overall strategy. This type of change often occurs in response to changes in the external environment, such as shifts in market trends, technological advancements or competitive pressures.

Structural change: Structural change involves alterations to the organisational structure, including changes in reporting relationships, job roles, departmental configurations or the introduction of new processes or systems. This type of change aims to improve efficiency, streamline operations or adapt to evolving business needs.

Cultural change: Cultural change involves transforming the values, beliefs, norms and behaviours within an organisation. This type of change is often necessary to align the organisation's culture with its strategic objectives, foster innovation and collaboration or address issues such as resistance to change or lack of diversity and inclusion.

Technological change: Technological change involves adopting, implementing or upgrading technologies within an organisation. This type of change can range from the introduction of new software applications or tools to the implementation of advanced manufacturing processes or automation systems.

Process change: Process change involves making modifications to the way work is done within an organisation. This could include redesigning workflows, standardising procedures or implementing lean or agile methodologies to improve efficiency, quality or customer satisfaction.

People change: People change focuses on developing employees' skills, capabilities and attitudes to support organisational objectives. This type of change may involve training and development initiatives, leadership coaching, performance management systems or talent management strategies.

Incremental change: Incremental change involves making small, gradual adjustments to existing processes, systems or strategies over time. This approach allows organisations to continuously improve and adapt to changing circumstances without causing significant disruption.

Transformational change: Transformational change involves fundamental and far-reaching shifts in the organisation's structure, culture, processes or strategy. This change is often driven by the need to respond to disruptive forces, capitalise on new opportunities or address significant challenges facing the organisation.

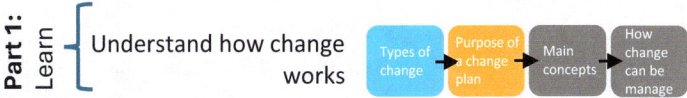

Learn:

Understanding the Purpose of a Change Plan and Grasping the Main Components

Learn: Understanding the Purpose of a Change Plan and Grasping the Main Components

The purpose of a change plan is to outline a structured approach for implementing and managing changes within an organisation or a project. It serves as a roadmap to guide stakeholders through the transition process, ensuring that changes are effectively communicated, understood and integrated. Ultimately, the objective of a change plan is to support organisational growth, improvement and adaptation in response to evolving internal or external factors.

A change plan typically encompasses these components:

1. **Schedule and detailed plan:** Outlines the timeline and specific actions required to implement the proposed changes. It includes milestones, deadlines and tasks assigned to individuals or teams. Tasks and activities include audience analysis, change impacts analysis, communications and training activities

2. **Strategy:** Details the overarching approach and goals of the change initiative.

3. **Audience analysis:** Involves identifying and understanding the various stakeholders affected by the changes. It includes analysing their needs, concerns, attitudes and potential reactions to ensure tailored communications and engagement strategies.

4. **Change impacts analysis:** Assesses the potential effects of the proposed changes on different aspects such as processes, systems, roles and culture. It helps anticipate challenges and plan mitigation strategies.

5. **Communications and engagement plan:** Outlines how information about the changes will be communicated to stakeholders. It includes messaging, channels, frequency and methods of feedback and involvement to ensure effective communication and buy-in.

6. Training plan: Details the training and development activities required to equip individuals with the knowledge, skills and resources to adapt to the changes successfully. It may include workshops, seminars, e-learning modules or on-the-job training.

7. Risk register: Identifies potential risks and obstacles that could impact the success of the change initiative. It includes an assessment of the likelihood and severity of each risk, as well as mitigation strategies to minimise their impact.

These components work together to provide a structured and comprehensive framework for planning, implementing and managing change within an organisation. Each component is essential for addressing different aspects of the change process and ensuring successful outcomes.

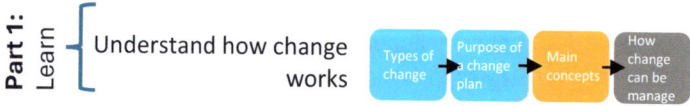

Part 1: Learn — Understand how change works

Types of change → Purpose of a change plan → Main concepts → How change can be manage

Learn:

Understanding the Main Concepts and Methodologies

Learn: Understanding the Main Concepts and Methodologies

The main players in the change:

In any change initiative, several key individuals play distinct roles in driving and facilitating the process. These main players are crucial for ensuring the successful implementation and adoption of the proposed changes.

Change sponsors are typically senior leaders or executives within the organisation who have the authority and resources to support and champion the change initiative. They provide strategic direction, allocate resources and endorse the change effort at the highest levels of the organisation. Change sponsors are responsible for articulating the vision for change, communicating its importance to stakeholders and removing obstacles that may hinder progress.

Change leaders are individuals tasked with overseeing and managing the day-to-day execution of the change initiative. They may include project managers, department heads or other middle managers who have direct responsibility for implementing the changes within their respective areas of influence. Change leaders are responsible for developing detailed plans, coordinating activities, monitoring progress and addressing any issues or challenges that arise during the change process. They serve as the primary drivers of the change effort, working closely with change sponsors to translate the vision into actionable plans and deliver tangible results.

Change champions are passionate advocates and influencers who are dedicated to promoting and supporting the change initiative within their respective teams or departments. They may not hold formal leadership positions but possess credibility, enthusiasm and influence among their peers. Change champions play a crucial role in mobilising support, building momentum and fostering a positive attitude towards change among their colleagues. They actively communicate the benefits of the change, address concerns and help overcome resistance by serving as role models and trusted advisors. Change champions often act as liaisons between change leaders and frontline employees, helping bridge the gap and ensuring effective communication and engagement throughout the organisation.

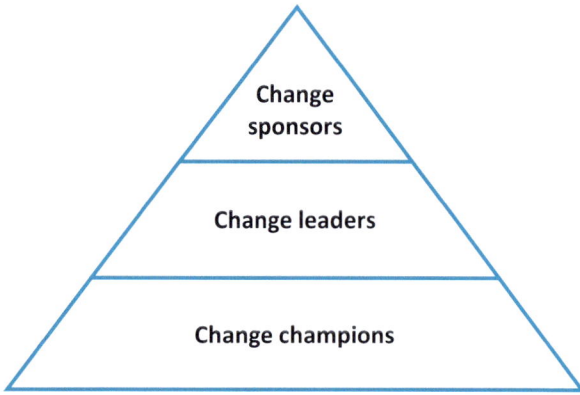

Examples of change management methodologies

There isn't a one-size-fits-all methodology for addressing organisational change; the choice depends on the specific type of change and the desired outcomes. Two commonly used methodologies are ADKAR[1] and the Kübler-Ross Change Curve[2]. These approaches offer different frameworks for understanding and managing change within an organisation.

ADKAR

The ADKAR model was developed nearly two decades ago by Prosci founder Jeff Hiatt after studying the change patterns of more than 700 organisations. It focuses on five key elements: Awareness, Desire, Knowledge, Ability and Reinforcement. This model helps individuals navigate through the stages of change by addressing their awareness of the need for change, desire to participate, knowledge of how to change, ability to implement change and reinforcement to sustain change.

Later, you will discover how to implement the ADKAR model across various aspects of your change plan. By aligning the ADKAR model with different phases of the project, you can systematically address the individual needs of stakeholders throughout the change process, ultimately increasing the likelihood of successful implementation and adoption.

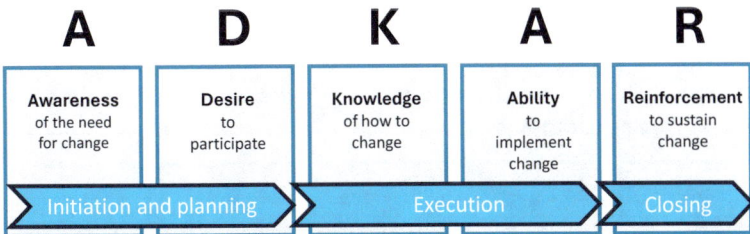

A	D	K	A	R
Awareness of the need for change	**Desire** to participate	**Knowledge** of how to change	**Ability** to implement change	**Reinforcement** to sustain change
Initiation and planning		Execution		Closing

This example illustrates how ADKAR elements can align with different phases of a project as stakeholders navigate through the process of change.

1 The Prosci "ADKAR Model". Prosci, n.d., www.prosci.com/adkar/adkar-model
2 "Kübler-Ross Change Curve". "Elisabeth Kübler-Ross FOUNDATION", n.d., https://www.ekrfoundation.org/5-stages-of-grief/change-curve/

Kübler-Ross Change Curve

The Kübler-Ross Change Curve, also known as the Five Stages of Grief model, is a psychological framework that describes the emotional stages individuals may experience when faced with significant change. Originally developed to understand the stages of grief experienced by terminally ill patients, it has been adapted to explain how people respond to various types of change, including organisational change.

The five stages outlined in the Kübler-Ross Change Curve are:

1. **Denial:** Initially, individuals may deny the reality of the change and may resist accepting it. They may feel shock, disbelief or even a sense of numbness.

2. **Anger:** As the reality of the change sets in, individuals may become frustrated, resentful or angry. They may direct their anger towards those responsible for the change or towards the situation itself.

3. **Bargaining:** In this stage, individuals may attempt to negotiate or make deals to avoid or minimise the impact of the change. They may seek ways to regain control or revert to the previous state.

4. **Depression:** As the full impact of the change becomes apparent, individuals may experience feelings of sadness, helplessness or loss. They may withdraw, lose interest in activities or struggle with low energy levels.

5. **Acceptance:** In the final stage, individuals come to terms with the change and begin to adapt to the new reality. They may feel a sense of calm, understanding or resolution and may start to explore opportunities for growth or acceptance of the change.

It's important to note that not everyone progresses through these stages in a linear fashion and individuals may revisit certain stages multiple times before reaching acceptance.

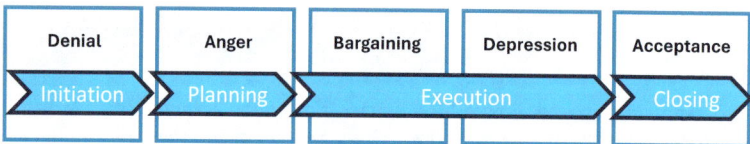

Denial	Anger	Bargaining	Depression	Acceptance
Initiation	Planning	Execution		Closing

This example illustrates how the emotional stages described in the Kübler-Ross Change Curve can align with different phases of a project as stakeholders navigate through the process of change.

Understand how change works

| Types of change | Purpose of change plan | Main concepts | How change can be manage |

Learn:

Understanding How Change Can Be Managed

Learn: Understanding How Change Can Be Managed

≡ Managing people through change involves the following key considerations:

Recognise individual reactions: Acknowledge that everyone responds differently to change and at their own pace. It's essential to understand the various emotional responses and provide support accordingly.

Facilitate communication: Communication is vital during times of change. Encourage open dialogue, seek input and provide opportunities for feedback to empower individuals and alleviate concerns.

Address resistance: Acknowledge that some individuals may resist change due to perceived threats. Provide clear information, facts and figures to address misconceptions and ease apprehensions.

Maintain engagement: Even high-performing employees may become disengaged during periods of change. Ensure ongoing engagement through formal and informal communication, timely updates and repetition of key messages.

Address concerns directly: Be transparent and realistic about the challenges and negative impacts of change. Address questions and concerns directly, escalating issues when necessary and providing support where needed.

≡ Incorporate planned engagement actions and change management interventions to support change and minimise resistance:

- Assign change leads to proactively engage with each area of change and identify potential resistance.

- Engage with individuals resistant to change, explaining the rationale behind the changes and the benefits for both individuals and the organisation.

- Provide timely and consistent communication through leaders, supported by information packs to ensure clear messaging.

- Engage influential individuals within the community (Change Champions) to drive change and adoption.

	Learn	Create / Analyse	Finalise
Schedule and plan	Learn — Step 1	Create — Step 2	Finalise — Step 15
Audience analysis	Learn — Step 3	Analyse — Step 4	Finalise — Step 13
Change impacts analysis	Learn — Step 5	Analyse — Step 6	Finalise — Step 12
Communications plan	Learn — Step 7	Create — Step 8	Finalise — Step 11
Training plan	Learn — Step 9	Create — Step 10	Finalise — Step 14

Part 2: Do

Step 1:

Learn about the Change Management Plan and Schedule

Step 1: Learn about the Change Management Plan and Schedule

The change management plan is the central hub for monitoring and managing your actions and tasks. The change management schedule and plan are aligned with the phases and tasks of the project plan but include unique steps during various project stages. You can utilise the template provided to document your plan or feel free to use any other tools that suit your preferences.

	Display Week:	1		Feb 26, 2024	

TASK	ASSIGNED TO		START	END	M T W T F S S M
Develop change management plan and strategy					
High level	Open				
Detailed	Open				
Communications and engagement					
Plan – High level	Open				
Plan – Detailed	Open				
Item 1	Open				
Item 2	Open				
Item 3	Open				
Item 4	Open				
Item 5	Open				
Item 6	Open				
Item 7	Open				
Audience analysis					
Define stakeholders	Open				
Define user groups	Open				
Define personas	Open				
Define roles	Open				
Assign users to the groups	Open				
Assign users to the groups – update	Open				
Campions					
Identify (BG, location, user group)	Open				
Confirm dates and workload	Open				
Confirm names with managers	Open				
Meeting: Induction	Open				
Training					
Plan – High level	Open				
Plan – Detailed	Open				
Training materials and resources	Open				
End user training	Open				
Process mapping					
High level	Open				
Detailed	Open				
Change impacts and gaps					
High level	Open				
Detailed (by area and user group)	Open				
Go-live					
User readiness review	Open				
Go-live activities	Open				
Survey					
Survey	Open				
Post Go-live					
Post Go-live activities	Open				

Change activities per project phase

Typically, you will need to complete these change management activities during various project phases to ensure successful change management.

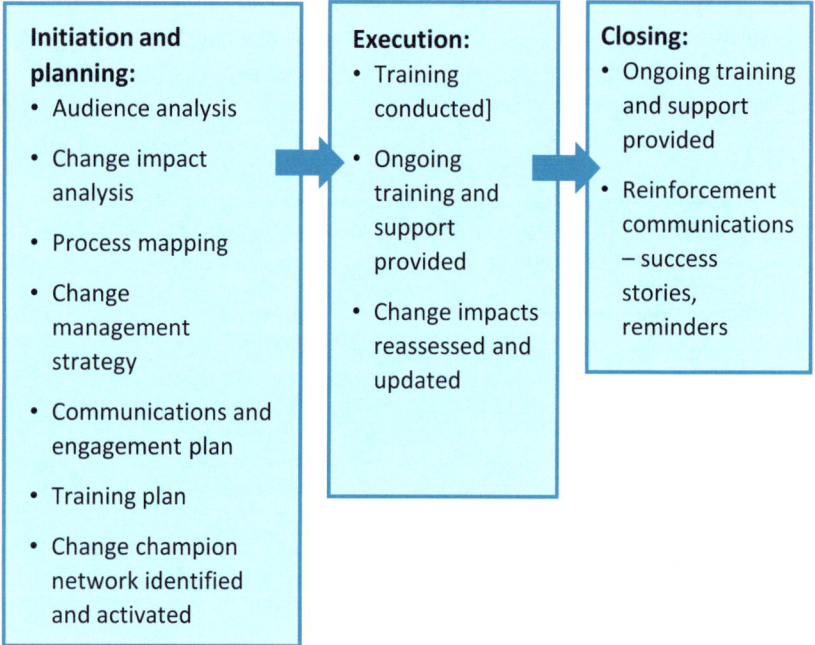

Initiation and planning:
- Audience analysis
- Change impact analysis
- Process mapping
- Change management strategy
- Communications and engagement plan
- Training plan
- Change champion network identified and activated

Execution:
- Training conducted]
- Ongoing training and support provided
- Change impacts reassessed and updated

Closing:
- Ongoing training and support provided
- Reinforcement communications – success stories, reminders

Part 2: Do

	Learn	Create	Finalise
Schedule and plan	Step 1	Step 2	Step 15
Audience analysis	Learn / Step 3	Analyse / Step 4	Finalise / Step 13
Change impacts analysis	Learn / Step 5	Analyse / Step 6	Finalise / Step 12
Communications plan	Learn / Step 7	Create / Step 8	Finalise / Step 11
Training plan	Learn / Step 9	Create / Step 10	Finalise / Step 14

Step 2:
Create a Draft Change Plan

Step 2: Create a Draft Change Plan

Sequence and timing of change management activities (example)

Activity	Sequence and project phase
Develop a change management plan and strategy	
High-level	*1. This is the draft you are creating as a part of this step. INITIATION AND PLANNING*
Detailed	*21. EXECUTION*
Communications and engagement	
Plan – High-level	*8. Draft plan (see Step 7 of this guide). INITIATION AND PLANNING*
Plan – Detailed	*13. INITIATION AND PLANNING*
Item 1	*14. INITIATION AND PLANNING*
Item 2 …	*16. EXECUTION*
Audience analysis	
Define stakeholders	*2. See Step 5 of this guide. INITIATION AND PLANNING*
Define user groups	*3. INITIATION AND PLANNING*
Define personas	*4. INITIATION AND PLANNING*
Define roles	*5. INITIATION AND PLANNING*
Assign users to the groups	*15. EXECUTION*
Assign users to the groups – update	*22. EXECUTION*
Campions	
Identify (team, location, user group)	*6. INITIATION AND PLANNING*
Confirm dates and workload	*11. INITIATION AND PLANNING*
Confirm names with managers	*12. INITIATION AND PLANNING*
Training	
Plan – High-level	*10. Draft plan (see Step 8 of this guide). INITIATION AND PLANNING*
Plan – Detailed	*19. EXECUTION*
Training materials and resources	*20. EXECUTION*
End-user training	*23. EXECUTION*
Process mapping	
High-level	*9. INITIATION AND PLANNING*
Detailed	*17. EXECUTION*
Change impacts and gaps	
High-level	*7. High-level analysis (see Step 6 of this guide). INITIATION AND PLANNING*
Detailed (by area and user group)	*18. EXECUTION*
Go-live	
User-readiness review	*24. EXECUTION*
Go-live activities	*25. EXECUTION*
Survey	
Survey	*26. CLOSING*

Once this step is completed, you will have:

A draft plan and schedule encompassing all activities with indicative dates. These activities are detailed in the template provided.

Part 2: Do

	Schedule and plan		
Learn Step 1	Create Step 2	Finalise Step 15	

Schedule and plan — Learn Step 1, Create Step 2, Finalise Step 15

Audience analysis — Learn Step 3, Analyse Step 4, Finalise Step 13

Change impacts analysis — Learn Step 5, Analyse Step 6, Finalise Step 12

Communications plan — Learn Step 7, Create Step 8, Finalise Step 11

Training plan — Learn Step 9, Create Step 10, Finalise Step 14

Step 3:

Learn about Different Methods to Analyse the Audience

Step 3: Learn about Different Methods to Analyse the Audience

There are three fundamental methods for analysing the audience, each offering unique insights and strategies for effective adaptation: by stakeholder groups, by user groups and by personas.

Stakeholders (used for communication)	User groups (used for training and communication)	Personas (used for engagement)
Who they are: Stakeholders are individuals or groups with an interest in or influence over the proposed changes. This includes individuals, groups, departments or organisations both internal and external to the company. You should consider stakeholders at various levels of the organisation hierarchy and across different functional areas.	**Who they are:** User groups represent individuals or teams who will directly interact with the changes introduced by the initiative. This could include end-users of a new software system, employees affected by process changes or customers experiencing changes in service delivery.	**Who they are:** Personas are fictional representations of typical users or stakeholders based on demographic, psychographic and behavioural data. Personas describe an overall mindset or attitude to change and can help you identify resistors or potential champions.
Example: Internal – employees, management team, board of directors, departments. External – customers, suppliers, partners, regulatory bodies, community. Other – investors, media, public, competitors	**Example:** Software Implementation – new CRM end-users, system administrators. Process optimisation – frontline/assembly line workers, supervisors. Service delivery – customers, client-facing employees.	**Example:** Ambassadors/champions = engaged, bystanders or sceptics = on the fence, challengers = disengaged.

Part 2: Do

Schedule and plan — Learn Step 1 → Create Step 2, Finalise Step 15

Audience analysis — Learn Step 3 → Analyse Step 4, Finalise Step 13

Change impacts analysis — Learn Step 5 → Analyse Step 6, Finalise Step 12

Communications plan — Learn Step 7 → Create Step 8, Finalise Step 11

Training plan — Learn Step 9 → Create Step 10, Finalise Step 14

Step 4:

Analyse the Audience

Step 4: Analyse the Audience

1. Analyse stakeholders

Step 1. Identify and create a list of stakeholder groups: Start by making a list of all potential stakeholders who could be impacted by the change.

Stakeholder group
Finance team
Leadership team

Step 2. Map stakeholders to their level of interest and influence: Create a stakeholder matrix to visualise their level of influence and interest in the change (high, medium, low).

Stakeholder group	Interest	Influence
Finance team	High	Medium
Leadership team	Low	High

Step 3. Map stakeholders to the audience: Work with an organisational chart to assign the audience to stakeholder groups. Please note that stakeholders can also include people outside the project.

Stakeholder group	Interest	Influence	Name
Finance team	High	Medium	John Doe
Leadership team	Low	High	Jane Smith

Step 4. Analyse stakeholder needs and expectations: Conduct interviews, surveys or focus groups to gather information about needs, concerns, expectations and objectives related to the change.

Stakeholder group	Interest	Influence	Name	Needs and expectations notes
Finance team	High	Medium	John Doe	Note
Leadership team	Low	High	Jane Smith	Note

What this information will be used for:
Creation of your communications plan, managing stakeholder relationships, adapting strategies based on stakeholder feedback.

Once this step is completed, you will have:
- A list of stakeholder groups mapped to their level of interest and influence
- A draft map of the audience to the stakeholder groups
- Notes against each stakeholder group about their needs and expectations

These activities are detailed in the template provided.

🍴 2. Analyse user groups

Step 1. Identify and create a list of user groups: Start by making a list of all potential users who will directly interact with the changes introduced by the initiative.

User group
Drivers
Managers

Step 2. Map users to processes: Map user groups to business processes, process areas, functions, project components, etc., with which these users will directly interact, e.g., new payroll software for a delivery company (project), drivers (user group), timesheets (business process) and timesheets entry (process area).

User group	Process	Process area
Drivers	Timesheets	Timesheet entry
Managers	Timesheets	Timesheet review

Step 3. Map users to the audience: Work with an organisational chart to assign the audience to user groups.

User group	Process	Process area	Name
Drivers	Timesheets	Timesheet entry	John Doe
Managers	Timesheets	Timesheet review	Jane Smith

Step 4. Conduct user needs assessment: Engage with each user group to understand their current workflows, pain points and requirements.

User group	Process	Process area	Name	Workflows, requirements
Drivers	Timesheets	Timesheet entry	John Doe	Note
Managers	Timesheets	Timesheet review	Jane Smith	Note

ⅢⅢ What this information will be used for:

User group analysis will be used as a basis for the change impacts assessment and training plan.

ⅢⅢ Once this step is completed, you will have:

- A list of user groups mapped to their processes, process areas, project components, etc.
- A draft map of the audience to user groups
- Notes against each user group about their current workflows and requirements

These activities are detailed in the template provided.

ᵀᵀᵀᵀ 3. Analyse personas

Step 1. Create persona profiles: Start by making a list of all potential persona profiles based on their mindset and attitude to change, characteristics, goals, pain points, etc. It's very important to identify and include your champion's network in this step.

Persona
Persona 1 (champions)
Persona 2

Step 2. Identify champions: Champions within the network serve as influential advocates for the change initiative. They can effectively communicate the benefits of the change to their peers, helping to build buy-in and support across the organisation. They encourage others who may have questions, concerns or reservations about the change. Champions often have valuable insights and feedback based on their firsthand experience with the change initiative, which can inform adjustments and refinements to the implementation strategy. Champions can also play a role in training and mentoring others during the transition period. They can share best practices, guide how to effectively use new tools or processes and offer ongoing support to help individuals overcome any challenges they may encounter.

Persona	Stakeholders	User groups	Audience
Persona 1 (champions)	Stakeholder	User group	Person 1, Person 2
Persona 2	Stakeholder	User group	

Step 3. Map personas to stakeholders, user groups and audience: Within each user and stakeholder group, a spectrum of personas exists, each with unique characteristics and inclinations. For instance, within a specific user group, some individuals enthusiastically champion change initiatives, while others may express reservations or challenges. It's crucial to note that these differences are not about labelling individuals but about recognising their diverse perspectives.

⛭ What this information will be used for:

Persona profiles will be used to tailor change management strategies to the specific needs and preferences of each audience segment. The champions network will serve as a critical asset in change management, facilitating communication, support and engagement among individuals impacted by the change.

⛭ Once this step is completed, you will have:

- A list of persona profiles
- A list of potential change champions
- A map of individuals to personas, stakeholders and user groups

These activities are detailed in the template provided.

⅌⅌⅌⅌ 4. Audience analysis outputs

After completing "Step 4: Analyse the Audience", you should have a comprehensive matrix comprising a list of stakeholders, user groups and personas. Please refer to the template provided. Initially, rough assignments of individuals will be made to these groups. However, it's crucial to periodically review and adjust these assignments throughout the project to ensure accuracy and alignment with evolving needs. Final assignments will be made just before the go-live phase, particularly for training purposes. All communication and change activities will be structured around these groups moving forward.

Stakeh olders	Stakehol der level of influence and interest	User groups	User process, process area, etc.	Persona	Audience
Stakeh older A	High / med	User group A	Process 1	Persona 1 (champions)	Person 1, Person 2, Person 3
Stakeh older A	High / med	User group A	Process 1, 2	Persona 2	Person 7, Person 8, Person 9
Stakeh older A	High / med	User group A	Process 2	Persona 3	Person 10, Person 11, Person 12
Stakeh older A	High / med	User group B	Process 1, 4	Persona 1 (champions)	Person 1, Person 2, Person 16
Stakeh older A	High / med	User group B	Process 3	Persona 2	Person 17, Person 8, Person 18
Stakeh older A	High / med	User group B	Process 5, 10	Persona 3	Person 10, Person 19, Person 20
Stakeh older B	Med / low	User group A	Process 2, 15	Persona 1 (champions)	Person 1, Person 2, Person 3
Stakeh older B	Med / low	User group A	Process 6	Persona 2	Person 4, Person 5, Person 6
Stakeh older B	Med / low	User group A	Process 7	Persona 3	Person 13, Person 14, Person 15

Part 2: Do

	Learn	Create/Analyse	Finalise
Schedule and plan	Step 1	Step 2	Step 15
Audience analysis	Step 3	Step 4	Step 13
Change impacts analysis	Step 5	Step 6	Step 12
Communications plan	Step 7	Step 8	Step 11
Training plan	Step 9	Step 10	Step 14

Step 5:

Learn about the Change Impact Analysis

Step 5: Learn about the Change Impact Analysis

Change impact assessments involve analysing and understanding how a proposed change will affect various aspects of the organisation, including its people, processes, technology and culture

People:

- Roles and responsibilities: Determine how the change will impact the roles and responsibilities. Will there be changes to job descriptions, reporting structures or team dynamics?
- Skills and training needs: Assess whether employees possess the necessary skills to adapt to the change or if additional training will be required. Identify any skill gaps.
- Morale and engagement: Consider how the change may affect employee morale and engagement. Will the change be perceived positively or negatively by employees?

Processes:

- Workflow and efficiency: Analyse how the change will impact existing workflows and processes. Will the change streamline operations and improve efficiency, or will it introduce new complexities or bottlenecks?
- Integration with existing systems: Determine how the change will integrate with existing systems and processes within the organisation. Will modifications be needed to ensure seamless integration, or will new systems need to be implemented?
- Quality and performance: Assess how the change may affect the quality and performance of products or services delivered by the organisation. Will the change lead to improvements in quality and performance, or will there be risks of quality issues or performance gaps?

Technology:

- Infrastructure and systems: Evaluate how the change will impact existing technology infrastructure and systems. Will it be necessary to implement new technologies, or will modifications be needed to existing systems to support the change?
- Data management and security: Consider how the change will affect data management practices and security measures. Will there be changes to data storage, access controls or cybersecurity protocols?

- <u>User experience:</u> Assess how the change will impact the user experience for employees and customers interacting with technology systems. Will the change enhance usability and functionality, or will there be risks of user dissatisfaction or frustration?

Culture:
- <u>Values and norms:</u> Examine how the change may impact the organisation's values. Will the change align with existing cultural values, or will it require a shift in cultural mindset?
- <u>Resistance and acceptance:</u> Will employees embrace the change willingly or will there be pockets of resistance that need to be addressed?
- <u>Communication and collaboration:</u> Will the change facilitate better communication and collaboration, or will there be risks of silos or breakdowns in communication?

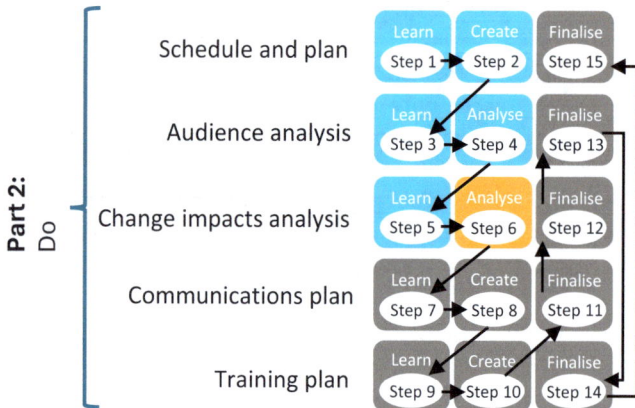

Part 2: Do

Schedule and plan — Learn Step 1 → Create Step 2 — Finalise Step 15

Audience analysis — Learn Step 3 → Analyse Step 4 — Finalise Step 13

Change impacts analysis — Learn Step 5 → Analyse Step 6 — Finalise Step 12

Communications plan — Learn Step 7 → Create Step 8 — Finalise Step 11

Training plan — Learn Step 9 → Create Step 10 — Finalise Step 14

Step 6:

Analyse Change Impacts

Step 6: Analyse Change Impacts

How to analyse change impacts

Quantifying change impacts involves measuring and assigning numerical values to the effects of a proposed change on various aspects of the organisation. While not all impacts can be easily quantified, many can be expressed in terms of key performance indicators (KPIs), metrics or other quantitative measures.

Step 1. Define measurement criteria: Start by defining the criteria or metrics that will be used to quantify the impacts of the change. These criteria should be relevant to the specific objectives of the change initiative, for example, complexity, frequency, novelty (high, medium, low).

Step 2. Identify key user groups that will be impacted by the change.

Step 3. Capture change impacts: Gather information, consider interviews and focus groups with key users and champions.

Step 4. Assign a level of impact and measurement for each process.

Step 5. Document current and future processes: Use flowcharts, process maps or lists of tasks required to complete processes.

Step 6. Aggregate and analyse data: Aggregate the impact scores across different measurement criteria or KPIs to provide an overall assessment of the change impacts. Analyse the data to identify patterns, trends and areas of strength or concern.

Step 7. Revisit and update change impact assessment throughout the duration of the project: Initial high-level change impact assessment will be useful for communications and detailed change impact assessment will be imperative for the training plan.

Example of a change impacts analysis

Change impact / change description	Process	Process area	User group impacted	Level of impacts			
				Change impact criteria 1. E.g., complexity (low=1, med=2, high=3)	Change impact criteria 2. E.g., novelty (low=1, med=2, high=3)	Change impact criteria 3. E.g., frequency (low=1, med=2, high=3)	Change impact score
Change 1	Process A	Area 1	User group 1	Low	Med	Low	1+2+1= 4
Change 2	Process A	Area 2	User group 1	Med	High	High	2+3+3= 8
Change 3	Process A	Area 2	User group 2	High	Low	Med	3+1+2= 6
Change 4	Process B	Area 3	User group 3	Low	Med	Med	1+2+2= 5
Change 5	Process C	Area 4	User group 2	Med	Low	High	2+1+3= 6
Change 6	Process C	Area 5	User group 4	High	High	High	3+3+3= 9

Example: *Change impacts with a change impact score below 5 are considered mild and may require user training and a low level of communication.*

Change impacts with a change impact score between 6 and 7 are considered moderate and will require user training, possible process adjustment and extensive communication.

Change impacts with a change impact score between 8 and 9 are considered severe and will require extensive user training focused on new ways of working, increased communication and engagement. These impacts should be noted in the risk register.

⌐. Change impacts analysis and other change activities

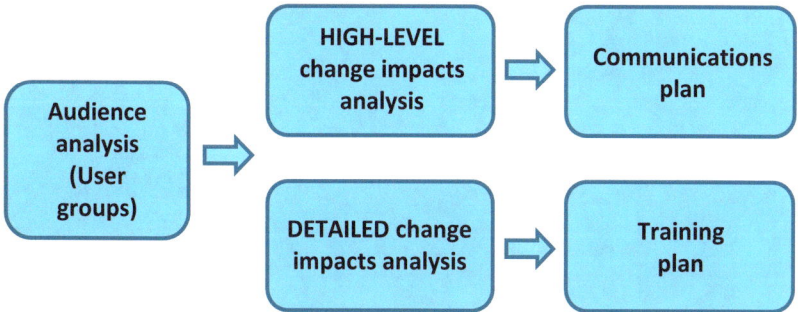

```
┌─────────────┐      ┌─────────────────┐      ┌─────────────────┐
│  Audience   │      │   HIGH-LEVEL    │      │ Communications  │
│  analysis   │ ⇒    │ change impacts  │ ⇒    │      plan       │
│   (User     │      │    analysis     │      │                 │
│  groups)    │      └─────────────────┘      └─────────────────┘
│             │ ⇒    ┌─────────────────┐      ┌─────────────────┐
└─────────────┘      │ DETAILED change │ ⇒    │    Training     │
                     │ impacts analysis│      │      plan       │
                     └─────────────────┘      └─────────────────┘
```

⌐. Once this step is completed, you will have:

- A list of high-level change impacts mapped to processes, process areas and user groups impacted
- An assessment of the change impact criteria and a calculation of the overall change impact score
- High-level process maps or lists of tasks – current and future state
- Notes against each change impact

These activities are detailed in the template provided.

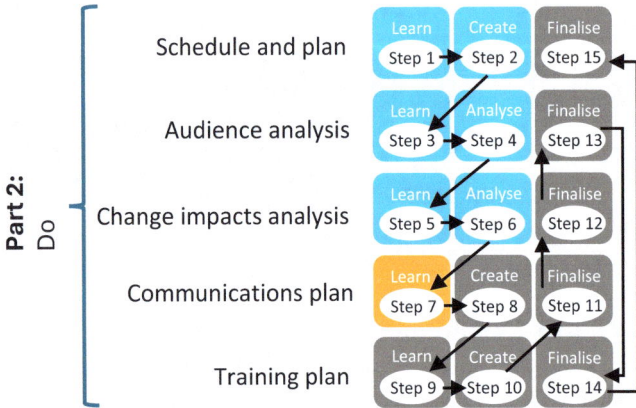

Part 2: Do

- Schedule and plan
- Audience analysis
- Change impacts analysis
- Communications plan
- Training plan

Learn / Create / Finalise grid:

Row	Learn	Create / Analyse	Finalise
Schedule and plan	Step 1	Step 2 (Create)	Step 15
Audience analysis	Step 3	Step 4 (Analyse)	Step 13
Change impacts analysis	Step 5	Step 6 (Analyse)	Step 12
Communications plan	Step 7	Step 8 (Create)	Step 11
Training plan	Step 9	Step 10 (Create)	Step 14

Step 7:

Learn about Communication & Engagement Principles and Components

Step 7: Learn about Communication & Engagement Principles and Components

Key components typically included in a communications and engagement plan

A communications and engagement plan for change is a strategic document that outlines how a project/organisation will communicate with and engage its audience throughout a change initiative.

1. Objectives: Clearly define the objectives of the communication and engagement efforts about the change initiative. This may include building awareness, gaining buy-in, managing resistance, providing updates, soliciting feedback or fostering a culture of transparency and collaboration.

2. Audience analysis: See Step 3 and Step 4 of this guide.

3. Key messages: Define the key messages that need to be communicated to the audience about the change initiative. These messages should clearly articulate the purpose, benefits, scope and timeline of the change, as well as address any potential concerns or questions that stakeholders may have.

4. Communication channels: Identify the most appropriate communication channels for reaching each stakeholder and user group. These may include face-to-face meetings, email updates, newsletters, intranet portals, social media, video messages, town hall meetings and other channels.

5. Communication timeline: Develop a timeline that outlines when and how each message will be communicated to the audience throughout the change initiative.

6. Engagement activities: Outline specific engagement activities designed to foster stakeholder and user participation and involvement in the change initiative. These may include workshops, training sessions, focus groups, working groups or other collaborative activities to solicit feedback, gather input and address concerns.

7. Responsibilities: Assign responsibilities for creating, delivering and managing communication & engagement activities to specific individuals or teams within the organisation.

8. Feedback mechanisms: Establish mechanisms for gathering feedback from the audience and responding to their questions, concerns and suggestions about the change initiative. These may include feedback forms, surveys, focus groups or designated contact points for inquiries.

9. Monitoring and evaluation: Define how the effectiveness of communication and engagement efforts will be monitored and evaluated. This may include tracking KPIs, conducting surveys, analysing feedback and making adjustments to the communication approach.

10. Contingency plans: Develop contingency plans to address unforeseen challenges or issues that may arise during the communication and engagement process. This ensures that communication efforts remain flexible and adaptable to changing circumstances.

Communication tactics

Clear and compelling messaging: Develop clear, concise and compelling messages that articulate the purpose, benefits and rationale behind the change initiative. Use language that resonates with the audience and emphasises the WIIFM (What's In It For Me) to address the audience's concerns and motivations.

Storytelling: Use storytelling techniques to communicate the vision and goals of the change initiative in a relatable and memorable way. Share success stories, testimonials and examples of how the change will positively impact individuals and the organisation as a whole.

Engagement forums: Create opportunities for two-way dialogue and engagement through forums such as town hall meetings, focus groups, workshops and feedback sessions. Encourage open and honest communication, listen to the audience's concerns and transparently address questions.

Leadership communication: Mobilise organisational leaders to champion the change initiative and communicate its importance to the audience. Leaders should lead by example, consistently reinforcing key messages and demonstrating commitment to the change through their actions and behaviors.

Multi-channel communication: Utilise a variety of communication channels and platforms to reach different stakeholder groups effectively. This may include face-to-face meetings, emails, newsletters, intranet portals, social media, video messages and other communication tools.

Change champions network: Establish a network of change champions who can serve as advocates for the change initiative within their respective teams or departments. Empower these individuals with the information, resources and support they need to drive the change.

Visual communication: Use visual aids such as infographics, charts, diagrams and videos to convey complex information and concepts clearly and engagingly. Visual communication can enhance understanding, capture attention and leave a lasting impression on the audience.

Celebration and recognition: Celebrate milestones, achievements and successes throughout the change process to reinforce positive behaviours and build momentum. Recognise individuals and teams for their contributions to the change initiative, fostering a culture of appreciation and motivation.

Align your communications plan with the ADKAR model

Awareness:
Tactic: Introduce the change initiative through various communication channels to create awareness among the audience.

How: Use meetings, emails, newsletters and intranet announcements to inform the audience about the upcoming change, its purpose and the expected impact.

Desire:
Tactic: Generate interest and enthusiasm for the change by highlighting its benefits and relevance to stakeholders.

How: Share success stories, case studies and testimonials to showcase the positive outcomes of similar changes.

Knowledge:
Tactic: Provide stakeholders with the information and resources they need to understand the change and its implications.

How: Offer training sessions, workshops and materials to educate the audience about the change initiative, its goals and how it will affect them.

Ability:
Tactic: Equip users with the skills and tools necessary to implement the change successfully.

How: Offer hands-on training, job aids and coaching sessions to help users develop the skills and confidence needed to adapt to the change.

Reinforcement:
Tactic: Sustain momentum and commitment to the change by reinforcing its importance and celebrating successes.

How: Use regular updates, town hall meetings and progress reports to reinforce key messages and maintain engagement over time.

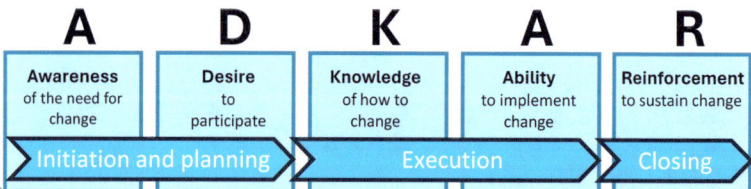

A	**D**	**K**	**A**	**R**
Awareness of the need for change	**Desire** to participate	**Knowledge** of how to change	**Ability** to implement change	**Reinforcement** to sustain change
Initiation and planning		Execution		Closing

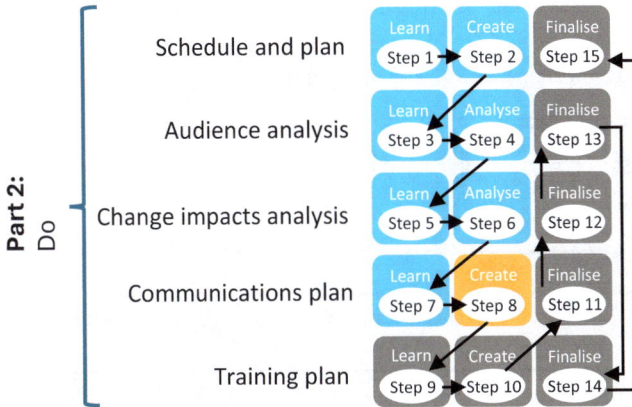

Part 2: Do

- Schedule and plan — Learn Step 1 → Create Step 2 → Finalise Step 15
- Audience analysis — Learn Step 3 → Analyse Step 4 → Finalise Step 13
- Change impacts analysis — Learn Step 5 → Analyse Step 6 → Finalise Step 12
- Communications plan — Learn Step 7 → Create Step 8 → Finalise Step 11
- Training plan — Learn Step 9 → Create Step 10 → Finalise Step 14

Step 8:

Create a Communications and Engagement plan

Step 8: Create a Communications and Engagement plan

Start drafting your communications plan

Step 1. Define the objectives.

Step 2. Develop and define key messages.

Step 3. Identify communication channels.

Step 4. Set up a communication timeline.

Step 5. Assign responsibilities and dates.

Step 6. Include engagement activities.

Type	Key message	Audience	Channel	Who	When	Status
Introduction	We are kicking off ... project	All staff	Email	Project owner	Date	In progress
...	...	Stakeholder / user group	Channel	...	Date	Status

Key items to be included in the communications plan

- Purpose of the change
- Benefits of the change (What's in it for me)
- Impact on stakeholders and users (change impacts)
- Support and resources available
- Timeline and the implementation plan (dates, project phases, training, go-live)
- Communication and engagement opportunities
- Leadership commitment and support
- Continuous improvement and feedback loop
- Celebrating successes and milestones
- Vision for the future
- Training activities
- Go-live activities

Key messages and timing

Key message	Example	Audience	When
Purpose of the change	Clearly articulate why the change is necessary and what problem or opportunity it aims to address. *Example: "The purpose of this change initiative is to streamline our processes, improve efficiency and enhance customer satisfaction."*	Everyone, separate messages to different groups	Initiation, planning
Benefits of the change	Highlight the positive outcomes and benefits that the change will bring to stakeholders and the organisation as a whole. *Example: "This change will result in cost savings, faster response times and higher-quality products/services."*	Everyone, separate messages to different groups	Planning, execution
Impact on stakeholders and users	Explain how the change will impact different stakeholder and user groups. *Example: "Employees will have access to new training opportunities and career advancement paths."*	Separate messages to different groups	Planning, execution

Key message	Example	Audience	When
Support and resources available	Assure stakeholders that support and resources will be provided to help them adapt to the change effectively. *Example: "We will offer training sessions, resources and support to assist employees in transitioning to the new system."*	Everyone, separate messages to different groups	Planning, execution
Timeline and implementation plan	Provide an overview of the timeline and implementation plan for the change initiative, including key milestones and stages. *Example: "The change will be rolled out in phases over the next six months, with training sessions scheduled for all staff members."*	Everyone	Initiation, planning, execution
Communication and engagement opportunities	Encourage stakeholders to participate in communication and engagement activities, such as town hall meetings, feedback sessions and focus groups. *Example: "We value your input and encourage you to share your thoughts, concerns and ideas throughout the change process."*	Everyone, separate messages to different groups	Planning, execution

Key message	Example	Audience	When
Leadership commitment and support	Demonstrate leadership commitment and support for the change initiative, reinforcing confidence in its success. *Example: "Our leadership team is fully committed to this change initiative and will provide guidance and support every step of the way."*	Everyone	Initiation, planning, execution
Continuous improvement and feedback loop	Emphasise the organisation's commitment to continuous improvement and the importance of feedback in refining the change initiative. *Example: "We welcome your feedback and will use it to make adjustments and improvements as needed to ensure the success of the change."*	Everyone	Planning, execution
Celebrating successes and milestones	Recognise and celebrate successes and milestones achieved throughout the change process to maintain momentum and motivation.	Everyone	Execution

Key messages and timing (continued)

Key message	Example	Audience	When
Vision for the future	Paint a picture of the future state and vision for the organisation once the change initiative is successfully implemented. *Example: "Together, we will create a more agile, innovative and resilient organisation that is well-positioned for future growth and success."*	Everyone	Execution, closure

Once this step is completed, you will have:

1. A draft communications plan:
- Objectives
- Key messages
- Channels
- Timeline
- Responsibilities
- Engagement activities

2. Communication activities linked/included in the change plan and schedule.

Communication plan activities are detailed in the template provided.

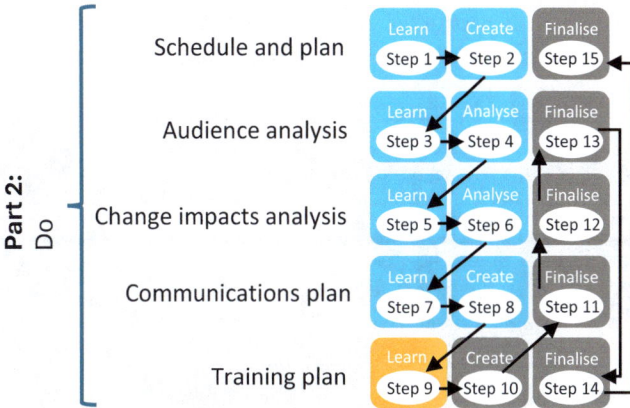

Part 2:
Do

	Learn	Create	Finalise
Schedule and plan	Step 1	Step 2	Step 15
Audience analysis	Learn Step 3	Analyse Step 4	Finalise Step 13
Change impacts analysis	Learn Step 5	Analyse Step 6	Finalise Step 12
Communications plan	Learn Step 7	Create Step 8	Finalise Step 11
Training plan	Learn Step 9	Create Step 10	Finalise Step 14

Step 9:

Learn about Training Plan Principles and Components

Step 9: Learn about Training Plan Principles and Components

Training plan components

The training plan is a structured document that outlines the approach, objectives, content and timeline for training users to adapt to a new change.

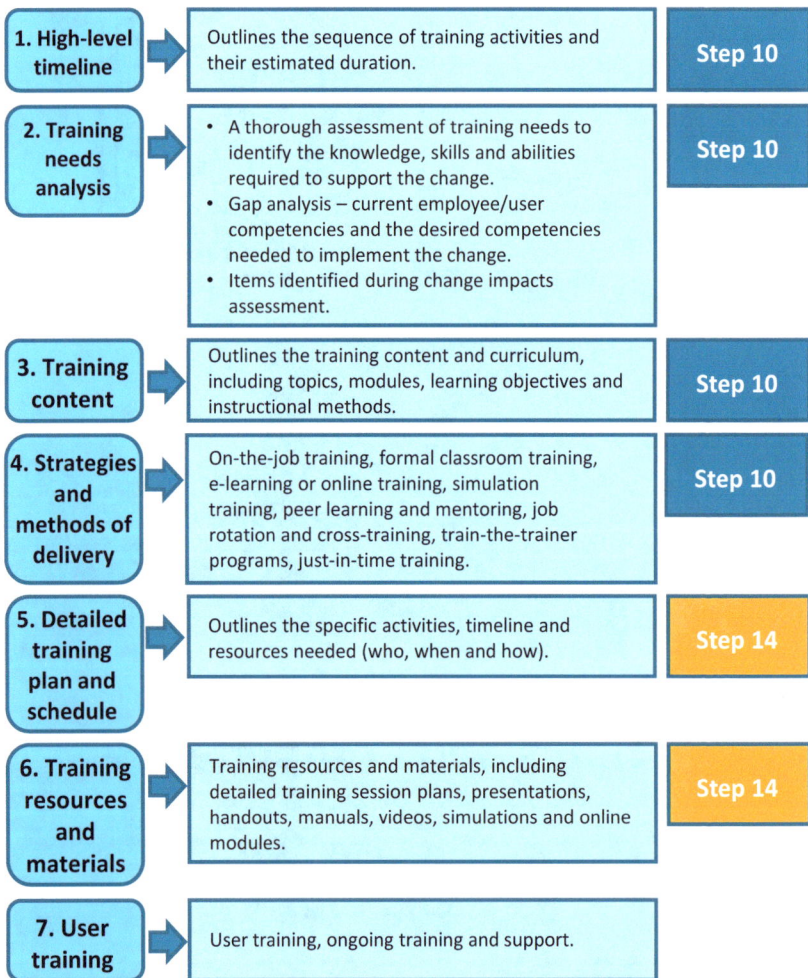

1. High-level timeline	Outlines the sequence of training activities and their estimated duration.	**Step 10**
2. Training needs analysis	• A thorough assessment of training needs to identify the knowledge, skills and abilities required to support the change. • Gap analysis – current employee/user competencies and the desired competencies needed to implement the change. • Items identified during change impacts assessment.	**Step 10**
3. Training content	Outlines the training content and curriculum, including topics, modules, learning objectives and instructional methods.	**Step 10**
4. Strategies and methods of delivery	On-the-job training, formal classroom training, e-learning or online training, simulation training, peer learning and mentoring, job rotation and cross-training, train-the-trainer programs, just-in-time training.	**Step 10**
5. Detailed training plan and schedule	Outlines the specific activities, timeline and resources needed (who, when and how).	**Step 14**
6. Training resources and materials	Training resources and materials, including detailed training session plans, presentations, handouts, manuals, videos, simulations and online modules.	**Step 14**
7. User training	User training, ongoing training and support.	

1. High-level timeline (complete in Step 10)

A high-level training timeline covers the sequence, estimated duration and the dates for these activities:

1. Create the high-level timeline

2. Conduct the training needs analysis

3. Define the training content

4. Define the strategy and methods of delivery

5. Prepare the detailed training plan and schedule

6. Prepare the training resources and materials

7. Conduct user training

2. Training needs analysis (complete in Step 10)

Assessment of training needs:

- Conduct a comprehensive assessment of the knowledge, skills and abilities required to support the change initiative. This assessment should cover various aspects of the change, including new processes, systems, tools and roles.

- Identify the specific areas where employees may need training to effectively adapt to the change and perform their roles successfully.

- Consider the diverse needs and preferences of different employee/user groups taking into account factors such as job roles, experience levels and learning styles.

Gap analysis:

- Perform a gap analysis to compare the current competencies of employees/users with the competencies needed to implement the change successfully.

- Identify any discrepancies or gaps between existing employee/user competencies and the skills and knowledge required to support the change.

- Determine the specific areas where additional training or development is needed to bridge these gaps and ensure that employees/users are adequately prepared for the change.

Other items to consider:
- Review the results of the change impacts assessment to identify specific training needs arising from the change initiative.
- Consider how the change will impact different aspects of user roles, responsibilities, workflows and interactions with systems or processes.
- Identify any new skills, knowledge or competencies that employees will need to acquire to adapt to the changes brought about by the initiative.

3. The training content (complete in Step 10)

Break down the training content into modules or topics based on the identified learning objectives.
Each module should focus on a specific aspect of the change initiative, such as new processes, tools, systems or job roles.

4. Strategies and methods of delivery (complete in Step 10)

On-the-job training: In this approach, employees learn new skills or procedures while performing their regular job duties. It allows for immediate application of newly acquired knowledge and skills in a real-world context. On-the-job training can be facilitated by supervisors, mentors or experienced colleagues.

Formal classroom training: This involves structured instructor-led training sessions conducted in a classroom or training facility. It provides a systematic approach to learning and allows for in-depth coverage of the material. Formal training sessions can be particularly useful for complex or technical topics that require a deeper understanding.

E-Learning or online training: E-learning platforms and online training modules provide flexible and accessible learning opportunities for employees. Employees can access training materials remotely, at their own pace and on their preferred devices. E-learning can include interactive modules, videos, quizzes and other multimedia elements to enhance engagement and retention.

Simulation training: Simulation-based training involves replicating real-world scenarios or environments to allow employees to practice and refine their skills in a risk-free setting. It provides hands-on experience and allows employees to experiment with different approaches and strategies. Simulation training can be particularly effective for high-risk or complex tasks.

Peer learning and mentoring: Peer learning and mentoring programs pair employees with more experienced colleagues who can provide guidance, support and feedback. They promote knowledge sharing, collaboration and the transfer of knowledge within the organisation. Peer learning and mentoring can be informal or formalised through structured mentoring programs.

Job rotation and cross-training: Job rotation involves temporarily assigning employees to different roles or departments to broaden their skills and perspectives. Cross-training involves training employees to perform tasks or duties outside of their primary role. Job rotation and cross-training help employees develop a diverse skill set and increase organisational flexibility.

Train-the-trainer programs: Train-the-trainer programs involve training a select group of employees to become trainers who can then deliver training to their peers. They leverage internal expertise and build capacity within the organisation to sustain training efforts over the long term. Train-the-trainer programs can be cost-effective and efficient for large-scale training initiatives.

Just-in-time training: Just-in-time training provides targeted training or support at the moment of need, often in the form of job aids, quick-reference guides or online resources. It addresses specific gaps encountered by employees in real time, minimising downtime and maximising productivity.

5. Detailed training plan and schedule (complete in Step 14)

- Develop a training schedule and timeline that outlines when and where training activities will take place.
- Consider factors such as the availability of trainers, facilities and resources, as well as the timing of key milestones in the change initiative.

6. Training resources and materials (complete in Step 14)

Based on the needs assessment, develop customised training and support materials to help user groups transition smoothly to the new processes or systems and address any issues or concerns that arise during the implementation phase.

1. Presentations: Create PowerPoint presentations or other visual aids to convey key concepts, processes and information related to the change initiative.

2. Handouts and manuals: Develop handouts, manuals or reference guides that participants can use to review training content and reinforce learning outside of training sessions. Include summaries of key concepts, step-by-step instructions and troubleshooting tips to help participants apply their learning in real-world scenarios.

3. Videos and multimedia content: Produce instructional videos or multimedia presentations to demonstrate processes, procedures or scenarios relevant to the change initiative.

4. Interactive learning modules: Develop interactive e-learning modules or online training courses that allow participants to engage with the training content at their own pace and convenience. Include interactive quizzes, activities and simulations to reinforce learning objectives and assess participants' understanding.

5. Job aids and quick reference guides: Create job aids, quick reference guides or cheat sheets that provide employees with easy access to key information, procedures or resources related to the change initiative.

6. Workbooks and worksheets: Develop workbooks or worksheets that participants can use to apply their learning during training sessions. Include exercises, activities and reflection prompts that encourage participants to actively engage with training content and reinforce their understanding.

7. Supplementary resources: Compile supplementary resources, such as articles, case studies or external links that provide additional context, insights or perspectives related to the change initiative.

! Accessibility considerations: Ensure that all training materials and resources are accessible to participants with diverse learning needs, including those with disabilities or language barriers.

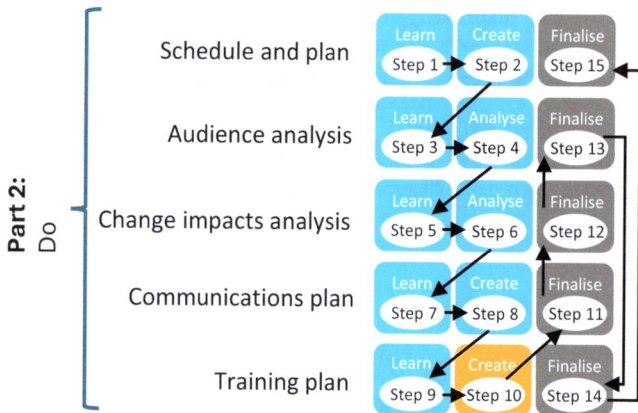

Part 2:
Do

Schedule and plan
- Learn — Step 1
- Create — Step 2
- Finalise — Step 15

Audience analysis
- Learn — Step 3
- Analyse — Step 4
- Finalise — Step 13

Change impacts analysis
- Learn — Step 5
- Analyse — Step 6
- Finalise — Step 12

Communications plan
- Learn — Step 7
- Create — Step 8
- Finalise — Step 11

Training plan
- Learn — Step 9
- Create — Step 10
- Finalise — Step 14

Step 10:

Create a Training Plan

Step 10: Create a Training Plan

1. Create a high-level plan and timeline

Create a high-level plan and timeline and link it to your overall change plan and schedule.

Item	When	Who	Status
Create a high-level timeline	Date		Open
Conduct a training needs analysis			
Define training content			
Define strategy and methods of delivery			
Prepare a detailed training plan and schedule			
Prepare training resources and materials			
Conduct user training			

2. Conduct training needs analysis

Use the Change impacts analysis table below to populate the training needs assessment and gaps.

Change impact / change description	Process	Process area	User group impacted	Training needs (knowledge, skills and abilities required to support the change)	Gaps (current employee / user competencies and the competencies needed to implement the change successfully)
Change 1	Process A	Area 1	User group 1		
Change 2	Process A	Area 2	User group 1		
Change 3	Process A	Area 3	User group 2		
Change 4	Process B	Area 4	User group 3		

3. Define training content

Use the Change impacts analysis table below to populate content – new processes, tools, systems or job roles required for training modules.

Change impact / change description	Process	Process area	User group impacted	Training needs	Gaps	Training content
Change 1	Process A	Area 1	User group 1	Need 1	Gap 1	
Change 2	Process A	Area 2	User group 1	Need 2	Gap 2	
Change 3	Process A	Area 3	User group 2	Need 3	Gap 3	
Change 4	Process B	Area 4	User group 3	Need 4	Gap 4	

4. Define strategy and methods of delivery

Use the Change impacts analysis table below to populate delivery methods.

Change impact / change description	Process	Process area	User group impacted	Training needs	Gaps	Training content	Delivery methods
Change 1	Process A	Area 1	User group 1	Need 1	Gap 1	Con tent 1	
Change 2	Process A	Area 2	User group 1	Need 2	Gap 2	Con tent 2	
Change 3	Process A	Area 3	User group 2	Need 3	Gap 3	Con tent 3	
Change 4	Process B	Area 4	User group 3	Need 4	Gap 4	Con tent 4	

Once this step is completed, you will have:

- A high-level training plan

- A training approach – Summary of training content and delivery methods that can be communicated to the audience

- A table outlining training needs and gaps, user groups that require training, training content and delivery methods

You will come back to training activities in Step 14 to finalise the training plan and compile training resources and materials.

Training plan activities are detailed in the template provided.

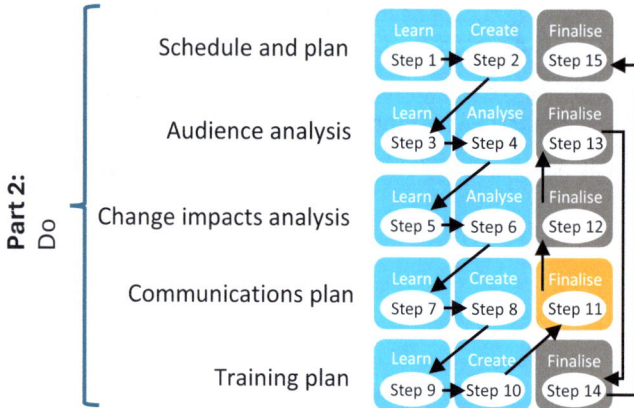

Part 2: Do

Schedule and plan
- Learn — Step 1
- Create — Step 2
- Finalise — Step 15

Audience analysis
- Learn — Step 3
- Analyse — Step 4
- Finalise — Step 13

Change impacts analysis
- Learn — Step 5
- Analyse — Step 6
- Finalise — Step 12

Communications plan
- Learn — Step 7
- Create — Step 8
- Finalise — Step 11

Training plan
- Learn — Step 9
- Create — Step 10
- Finalise — Step 14

Step 11:

Finalise the Communications and Engagement Plan

Step 11: Finalise the Communications and Engagement Plan

Add final details to your plan

- Training activities (approach and details)
- Update user groups if required
- Update stakeholder groups if required
- Update key messages if required
- Go-live activities

Once this step is completed, you will have:

1. A detailed communications plan:
- Objectives
- Key messages
- Channels
- Timeline
- Responsibilities
- Engagement activities
- Training activities
- Go-live activities

2. Communication activities linked/included in the change plan and schedule.

Communications plan activities are detailed in the template provided.

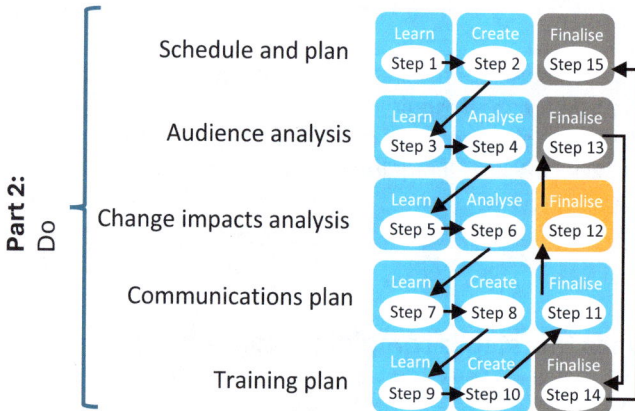

Part 2: Do

Schedule and plan	Learn / Step 1	Create / Step 2	Finalise / Step 15
Audience analysis	Learn / Step 3	Analyse / Step 4	Finalise / Step 13
Change impacts analysis	Learn / Step 5	Analyse / Step 6	Finalise / Step 12
Communications plan	Learn / Step 7	Create / Step 8	Finalise / Step 11
Training plan	Learn / Step 9	Create / Step 10	Finalise / Step 14

Step 12:

Finalise the Change Impacts Analysis

Step 12: Finalise the Change Impacts Analysis

⌐⌐ Add details

- Include any new change impacts identified.

- Describe all change impacts in detail.

- Detail current and future processes (elaborate on new processes, tools, systems or user/job roles).

⌐⌐ Once this step is completed, you will have:

1. Detailed change impacts:
- List of change impacts mapped to processes, process areas and user groups impacted
- Assessment of change impact criteria and calculation of overall change impact score
- Detailed process maps or lists of tasks – current and future state

2. Change impacts linked/included in the training plan.

3. Change impacts linked/included in the communications plan.

These activities are detailed in the template provided.

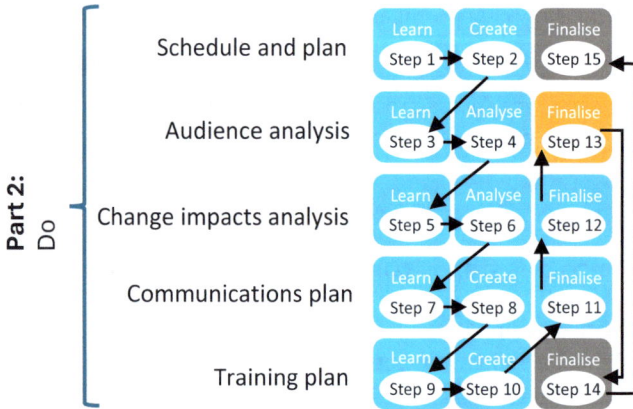

Part 2: Do

- Schedule and plan
  - Learn: Step 1 → Create: Step 2 | Finalise: Step 15
- Audience analysis
  - Learn: Step 3 → Analyse: Step 4 | Finalise: Step 13
- Change impacts analysis
  - Learn: Step 5 → Analyse: Step 6 | Finalise: Step 12
- Communications plan
  - Learn: Step 7 → Create: Step 8 | Finalise: Step 11
- Training plan
  - Learn: Step 9 → Create: Step 10 | Finalise: Step 14

Step 13:

Finalise the Audience Analysis

Step 13: Finalise the Audience Analysis

Assign individuals to the audience groups

- Map individuals to user groups (will be used for training and communications).
- Map individuals to stakeholder groups (will be used for communications and engagement).
- Map individuals to personas.

Once this step is completed, you will have:

- An updated list of individuals in the organisation mapped to user and stakeholder groups
- Users and user groups linked to the training plan
- User and stakeholder groups linked to the communications plan

These activities are detailed in the template provided.

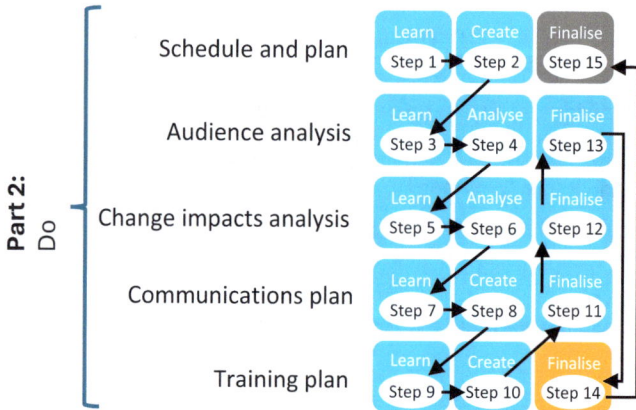

Part 2: Do

	Learn	Create	Finalise
Schedule and plan	Step 1	Step 2	Step 15
Audience analysis	Step 3	Step 4	Step 13
Change impacts analysis	Step 5	Step 6	Step 12
Communications plan	Step 7	Step 8	Step 11
Training plan	Step 9	Step 10	Step 14

Step 14:

Finalise the Training Plan

Step 14: Finalise the Training Plan

Set up a detailed training plan and schedule

- Develop a training schedule and timeline that outlines when and where training activities will take place.
- Consider factors such as the availability of trainers, facilities and resources as well as the timing of key milestones in the change initiative.

Training session	Description	Objectives	Trainees	Trainer	Duration	Date	Delivery method
Content		Linked to gaps, training needs and change impacts	User group				Classroom, on-the-job, etc.

Create training resources and materials

Develop customised training and support materials such as presentations, handouts & manuals, videos & multimedia content, interactive learning modules, job aids & quick reference guides, workbooks & worksheets and supplementary resources (see Step 9 of this guide).

Schedule user training

1. Use the latest audience to user groups mapping to schedule training sessions.
2. Communicate training schedule.
3. Provide flexibility.
4. Send reminders.
5. Evaluate and adjust if needed.
6. Provide follow-up and ongoing support.

Once this step is completed, you will have:

- A detailed training plan and schedule
- Training resources and materials
- A plan to schedule user training
- Link these activities to the communications plan
- Link these activities to the change plan

These activities are detailed in the template provided.

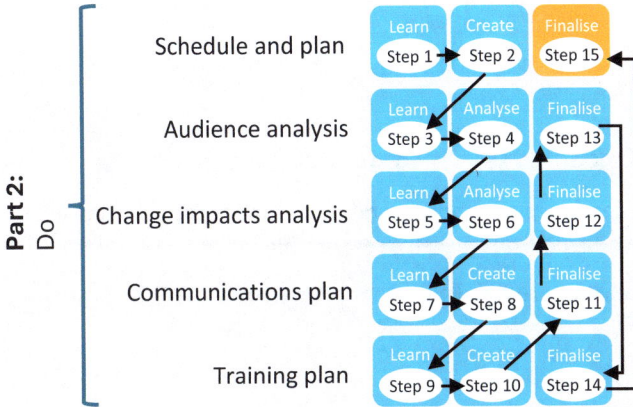

Part 2: Do

- Schedule and plan
  - Learn — Step 1 → Create — Step 2 → Finalise — Step 15
- Audience analysis
  - Learn — Step 3 → Analyse — Step 4 → Finalise — Step 13
- Change impacts analysis
  - Learn — Step 5 → Analyse — Step 6 → Finalise — Step 12
- Communications plan
  - Learn — Step 7 → Create — Step 8 → Finalise — Step 11
- Training plan
  - Learn — Step 9 → Create — Step 10 → Finalise — Step 14

Step 15:

Finalise the Change Plan and Schedule

Step 15: Finalise the Change Plan and Schedule

Add details

- Add all communications and engagement activities.
- Add all training activities.

Once this step is completed, you will have:

A final change plan and schedule encompassing all activities, dates, duration and individuals/teams responsible.

These activities are detailed in the template provided.

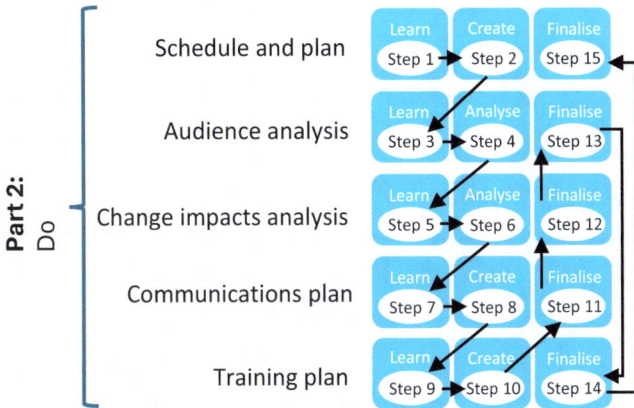

Part 2: Do

Schedule and plan — Learn: Step 1 → Create: Step 2 — Finalise: Step 15

Audience analysis — Learn: Step 3 → Analyse: Step 4 — Finalise: Step 13

Change impacts analysis — Learn: Step 5 → Analyse: Step 6 — Finalise: Step 12

Communications plan — Learn: Step 7 → Create: Step 8 — Finalise: Step 11

Training plan — Learn: Step 9 → Create: Step 10 — Finalise: Step 14

Well done!

You've completed all the essential steps to create a successful change plan. For additional information and guidance, please refer to the template provided.

Appendix

Appendix 1: High-level Change Plan Visual

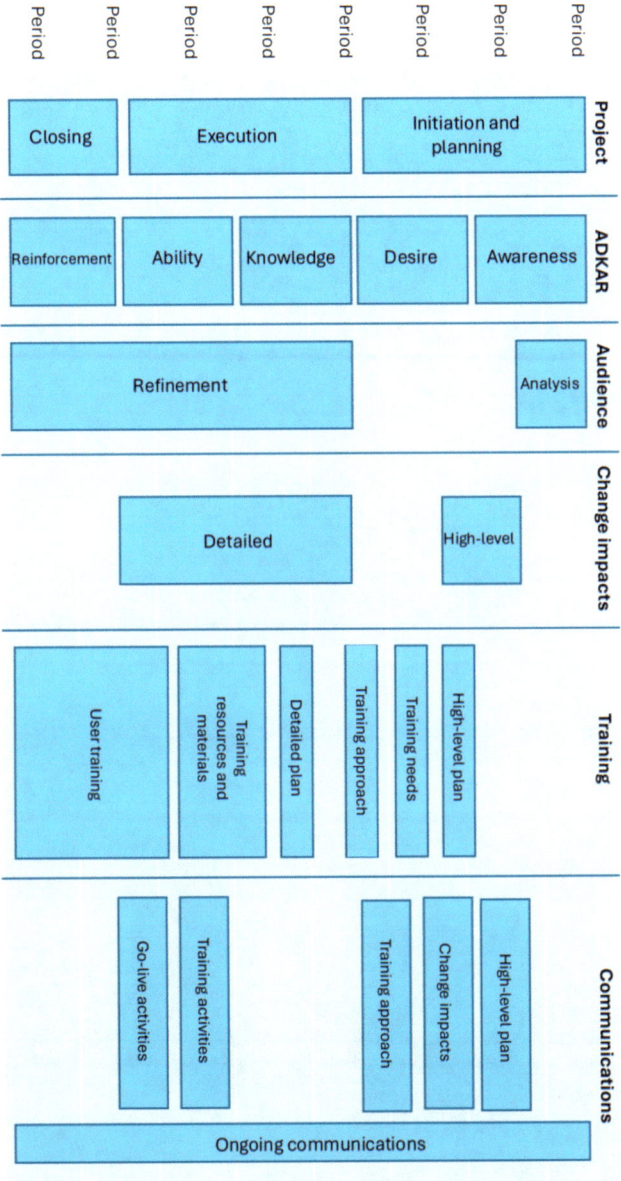

	Period	Period	Period	Period	Period	Period	Period	Period
Project	Closing		Execution			Initiation and planning		
ADKAR	Reinforcement	Ability		Knowledge		Desire		Awareness
Audience	Refinement							Analysis
Change impacts			Detailed			High-level		
Training	User training		Training resources and materials	Detailed plan	Training approach	Training needs	High-level plan	
Communications		Go-live activities	Training activities		Training approach	Change impacts	High-level plan	
	Ongoing communications							

Appendix 2: Template

Download the template by following this link:

• Template: Change management plan (incorporating Audience analysis, Change impact assessment, Communications and Training Initiatives)

https://rb.gy/f91xdx

Or
https://docs.google.com/spreadsheets/d/1PbGD2s62c75SjoxtO2LqTld Q8Frw3cUC/edit?usp=drive_link&ouid=113884894777213530999&rtp of=true&sd=true

Made in the USA
Columbia, SC
12 May 2025

57798647R00046